Freedom Friends

WRITTEN BY
Cameron Marasco

ILLUSTRATED BY
Sasha Beytler

A group of kids were very good friends.
They were inseparable through each school day's end.
They stood for the pledge of allegiance and prayer,
and they stood for each other — always with care.

Faith   Gracie   Ben   Thomas   George   Hope

Then one fine morning as the school day began, their teacher Ms. Dixon, said, "I'm a big fan of American history, the proud and the true — the brave men and women of the red, white and blue."

Ms. Dixon then smiled, as most teachers do,
"No, it means that those rights can't be taken from you.

Our American leaders are voted upon,
to protect these rights and the land that we're on."

The kids began to think of all they'd been told,
"What are these rights we've been given to hold?"
Ms. Dixon then answered, "What wonderful questions!
There are three main rights Thomas Jefferson mentions."

"They are Life, Liberty, and the Pursuit of Happiness;
he wrote in the Declaration of Independence.
To live your life free — chase your dreams as you please,
and to be able to choose any path as it leads."

Gracie's arm shot up, "Can I eat ice cream all day? 'Cause that would make me happy in a really big way!"

"You can do or be anything; you've got nothing to lose.
But there are consequences," said Ms. Dixon, "to the actions you choose".

"These rights come with great responsibility, you see.
Not all other countries have the right to be free.
Our country is special — unique in this way,
all people must stand for these freedoms to stay."

"See, these rights and these freedoms all can be lost.
If we as a people forget what it cost
for ALL people to be equal with their God-given rights.
If we don't learn and remember, we might lose sight."

"As Americans, strong and united, we can stand,
empowering one another as we walk hand in hand.

Each one of you has the power to be
the proud, and the brave, and especially the free."

"Wow!" exclaimed George, "Are those superpowers, too?"

"It can be if you work hard on the things you pursue." Ms. Dixon replied. "The pursuit is up to you — your work, your persistence — that's what makes it come true."

"This country gives you all the opportunity to create
the life of your dreams and it's never too late.
You can always get up and keep working on them,
to your fullest potential — follow any whim."

"And don't forget, children, with knowledge comes power.
If you think for yourself, those thoughts can empower –
so you can become all that you want to be.
You ARE an individual with life and liberty."

Freedom Friends: Words to Learn

Empower - to give power or authority to do something
Freedom - the ability to act without control by another person
Individual - person who thinks in their own original way
Inseparable - not to be apart, always together
Liberty - the state of being free
Opportunity - a situation that makes it possible to do something you want
Persistence - continuing to achieve something despite challenges
Pursue (pursuit) - the act of striving to accomplish something
Responsibility - something that is your duty or job to deal with
Unalienable - not capable of being taken away

Declaration of Independence Memory Work:

We hold these truths to be self-evident, that all men are created equal, that they are endowed by their Creator with certain unalienable Rights, that among these are Life, Liberty and the pursuit of Happiness.

The Thirteen Original Colonies of the United States of America:

Connecticut
Delaware
Georgia
Maryland
Massachusetts
New Hampshire
New Jersey
New York
North Carolina
Pennsylvania
Rhode Island
South Carolina
Virgina

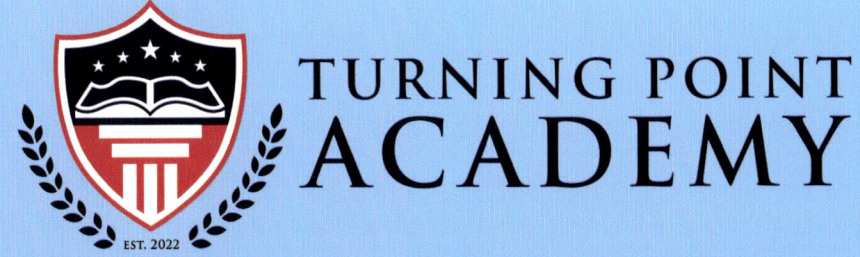

Turning Point Academy, a division of Turning Point USA, is dedicated to
RECLAIMING the education of our children,
REVIVING virtuous education focused on truth, goodness, and beauty, and
RESTORING God as the foundation of education.

We fulfill our mission in four ways:
1. Seeding Schools and Literacy Centers
2. Encouraging and Equipping Educators
3. Creating and Curating Curriculum
4. Establishing an Association of Likeminded Educators and Education Advocates.

If you are interested in learning more and joining the fight to reclaim, revive, and restore virtuous education, please visit us at www.TurningPointAcademy.com

 @freedomfriendsusa

 FreedomFriendsUSA

 freedomfriendsusa.com

Scan QR Below for Updates:
Freedom Friends Freebies

Illustrations:
www.behance.net/sashabeytler
sashabeytler@gmail.com

For my Aunt Christy,

My favorite teacher who encouraged my love for reading.

Thank you for always inspiring creativity and compassion in me...

To my husband, Mart, and my kids, Marli, Alaina, and Micah -

Thank you for your love and support through every step of this

journey.

Copyright © 2021 by Cameron Marasco

All rights reserved. No part of this book may be reproduced or used in any manner without written permission of the copyright owner except for the use of quotations in a book review.

Paperback edition August 2023

Book design and illustration by Sasha Beytler

ISBN 978-1-7376238-3-0

Printed in USA

Partnered with Turning Point Academy